Four Fundamentals

A Pocketbook for Self-Healing,
Self-Awakening, & Self-Liberation

PSYCHOLOGICAL INTEGRATION, CONSCIOUS EVOLUTION
& SPIRITUAL AWAKENING

Nicolya Christi

Copyright © 2020 by Nicolya Christi

All rights reserved. This book or any portion thereof
may not be reproduced or used in any manner whatsoever
without the express written permission of the publisher
except for the use of brief quotations in articles and book reviews.

'The ego/Self Fairytale' originally featured in '2012 A Clarion Call: Your Soul's Purpose in Conscious Evolution' - Nicolya Christi. Publisher Inner Traditions (2010)

'The Twelve Phases of Ascension' (up to phase nine) originally featured in '2012 A Clarion Call: Your Soul's Purpose in Conscious Evolution' - Nicolya Christi. Publisher Inner Traditions (2010)

'The 21 Arrows' originally mentioned in '2012 A Clarion Call: Your Soul's Purpose in Conscious Evolution' - Nicolya Christi. Publisher Inner Traditions (2010)

'The 21 Arrows' expanded upon in 'Contemporary Spirituality for an Evolving World' - Nicolya Christi. Publisher Inner Traditions (2013)

'The Diamond Heart Prayers' originally featured in 'Contemporary Spirituality for an Evolving World' - Nicolya Christi. Publisher Inner Traditions (2013)

Printed in the United States of America

First Printing, 2020

ISBN-13: 978-1-949001-64-8 print edition
ISBN-13: 978-1-949001-65-5 ebook edition

Waterside Productions

Waterside Productions
2055 Oxford Ave
Cardiff, CA 92007
www.waterside.com

Table of Contents

Introduction	v
The Four Fundamentals Overview	vii
A Blessing	ix
The Four Fundamental Teachings	1
Psychological Integration	3
Teaching One – The ego/Self Fairytale	3
Conscious Evolution	12
Teaching Two - The Twenty-One Arrows:	
A Map for Evolving Consciousnes	12
Spiritual Awakening	43
Teaching Three - The Twelve Phases of Ascension	43
Teaching Four - The Diamond Heart Prayers	55
About The Author	61

Introduction

Nicolya Christi presents Four Fundamentals for psychological integration, conscious evolution and spiritual awakening. In this pocketbook you will discover illuminating and transformational guidance on how to free yourself from the psychological and karmic ties that bind and awaken to the truth of *Who You Really Are* and live that as a day-to-day reality. Dip in and out of this unique little manual to experience cellular level healing, revelatory and evolutionary insights, metaphysical wisdom, and transcendent potentialities.

The Four Fundamentals Overview

- **The ego/Self Fairytale**

A unique approach to the healing and integration of the wounded and unintegrated ego and psychological shadow through storytelling in the form of an inspirational and revelatory fable.

- **The 21 Arrows – A Map for Evolving Consciousness**

An exclusive psycho-spiritual exploration of the First Nation Peoples' traditional Oral Wisdom Teaching - 'The Seven Dark, Seven Light, & Seven Rainbow Arrows'. This map for evolving consciousness was originally written by Nicolya in 2009. Recently, she has revised and re-edited it producing this newly updated account.

- **The Twelve Phases of Ascension**

A phenomenal psycho-spiritual and metaphysical trajectory revolving around the twelve instrumental 'gateways' of the Ascension Process. These phases are based on Nicolya's own personal experience as well as her penetrating perception and channelling of important information for our times. Insights from spiritual teachers Tashira Tachi-ren and Jasmuheen are included in some of the Phases.

- The Diamond Heart Prayers

Two very special Prayers that effectively and profoundly facilitate the healing, transformation and transcendence of historical, psychological, karmic, ancestral, and epigenetic psycho-spiritual patterns and conditioning.

A Blessing

This pocketbook is akin to a 'sacred medicine bundle'. The guidance contained herein can facilitate deep and profound healing and transformation. This portable friend offers itself as a soulful and inspiring companion to journey with as you navigate the path of psychological integration, conscious evolution and spiritual awakening.

May it prove to be a gift for your body, feelings and mind, and for your heart and soul.

May it act as an evolutionary catalyst to help guide you Home to your Self.

May it inspire you to align more fully with the truth of Who You Really Are and live that miraculous reality for the rest of your life.

And ... may it support you to remember why you are really here and where you are really from – **SOURCE-LOVE**.

The Four Fundamental Teachings

Psychological Integration

Teaching One – The ego/Self Fairytale

In 2009, I wrote a fable about the wounded ego and its reaction/response to the return of the once exiled Self seeking to reclaim its king-queendom. It is titled 'The Ego/Self Fairytale', and even though it was published in both my books - '2012: A Clarion Call' and 'Contemporary Spirituality for an Evolving World', I felt it was important to make it available in this Pocketbook. In essence, it is a deep and potentially transformative psycho-spiritual teaching. May all who read it recognize and benefit from the gift it wishes to offer in terms of psychological healing and integration, and may its invitation support you to come Home to your Self.

The Unintegrated Ego – A Misguided Yet Loyal Friend and Protector

The unintegrated ego is often referred to as the enemy of the True Self. It is viewed in this way because it keeps us locked in reaction, illusion, powerlessness, lack, insecurity, self-sabotaging and self-destructive patterns. In any deep and conscious psychological healing journey we *will* encounter the unintegrated ego, which, even though its reactions and actions are unconscious and misguided, acts in service to the True Self as a most loyal friend and protector. Yet the ego is concerned with survival and therefore will take all measures it views as necessary to negate or destroy anything that may threaten its position in the driving seat of an individual's life. However it's true purpose is misunderstood, for its ultimate role is to serve us. And here is where it becomes confused. In its wounding, its protection in the long-term is destructive, life-denying; yet, when it is healed, its wisdom is poetically supportive and life-serving

The True Self in Hiding

As infants, we incarnate as pure soul and it is at this time that our True Self is most present. This Authentic state of BEing is pure, undefended, and has a heart that is wide open. The ego first emerges when the True Self encounters anything other than unconditional love, gentleness, compassion, kindness, care, empathy, wisdom and grace, and/or when the world (caregiver/environment) is experienced as threatening or hostile.

The ego comes to the rescue of the True Self and puts up a 'warrior shield' of protection in front of it in order to save it from physical, emotional, mental and psychological harm or danger. It effects this through an armory of reaction, dishonesty, deceit, control, manipulation, sabotage, judgment, comparison, insensitivity, hostility, harshness, violence, fundamentalism, shyness, addiction, introversion, extroversion, glamour, bravado, guardedness, attack and defense. The ego steps into the role that the Self would have taken in terms of it engaging with day-to-day life had it been able to remain present in its purest and most unadulterated state; instead of needing to retreat to safety because of what it perceives as a life-threatening physical, emotional, mental and psychological environment.

And so the True Self goes into retreat and waits for the moment when the immediate psycho-spiritual environment poses little to no danger and is therefore sufficiently conducive for its re-emergence. The True Self can be likened to a King or a Queen of our being, and the ego as its most gallant knight. Whereas the ego would ride full charge into battle fully armed and with sword held high, the True Self is equipped only with words of peace and a grail overflowing with love. But the ego has forgotten that it is a knight or handmaiden and mistakenly believes it is the Sovereign of the Realm of Self.

The re-emergence of the True Self will often occur during mid to later life. Or it can take lifetimes for it to return as Emperor or Empress of the Kingdom/Queendom of Self. It is not necessary for the world to be calling it out due to an alignment with its purity. Indeed, it need only be one, or more, of similar pure heart to call it out of hiding. Yet all the while the True Self is in hiding, the unintegrated ego remains in the driving seat of our lives. Eventually, however, after building layer upon layer of barricades of defense, the ego begins to forget that the True Self ever existed and that its own role was to protect and serve the True Self. Ego is instinctual, not intuitive, and will always react not *respond*. It has developed sophisticated strategies, which keep it locked in survival mentality and set on one path - survival - at all costs. It mistakenly believes that it is the Sovereign of the Realm of Self, and, meanwhile, the true Regent - the True Self - remains hidden from the world.

The True Self is pure Unconditional Love and all that is wholesome and balanced, integrated and fair, gentle and wise and evolved and enlightened within us. This state of being never changes regardless of what unfolds in our lives. The fourteenth century philosopher Paracelsus shared that *inside each one of us is a special piece of heaven whole and unbroken.* This is the True Self and no matter what trauma stories may have occurred in our lives it will resurrect when we have explored, understood, healed and integrated the wounded ego/knight/handmaiden, which is driven by fear.

Adapted self – Authentic Self

In psychological terms, the ego is regarded as the *adapted self*, and the True Self as the *Authentic Self*. It is the 'adapted self' that most people mistakenly believe is who they really are. Over time, sub-personalities and identities are formed which are ego-bound and work against the need to confront and heal the deepest psychological-historical wounds within us. The first step towards *self*-healing and integration is to understand and acknowledge the role that the wounded ego has played in our lives in order to appreciate how it has served us well in ensuring our psychological and physical survival; even if the events we have experienced have caused great suffering to ourselves and others in service of our own physical, emotional and mental survival.

There comes a point on the path of healing when the True Self is ready to re-emerge and it is at this point that the ego becomes aware and takes immediate reactive steps. In fear, it devises what it believes to be failproof defenses and strategies. An example of this is when an individual whose heart may have been defended suddenly falls in love. The unintegrated ego will view anything that awakens the heart as a threat to its own survival, and therefore immediately reacts to defend against the emerging Self and the danger it believes this will pose to itself. Many a promising romantic love has fallen at the first hurdle, or later, due to the reaction of the unintegrated ego.

As the True Self begins its journey towards actualization it will encounter the ego and its defenses. This can equate to a feeling of one's life, or aspects of it, breaking down due to the unconscious force of defense (shadow material) that can erupt to the surface; examples of this are fear, anger, blame, shame, rage, worthlessness, inertia, fatigue, grief, mental overwhelm and physical and emotional pain, all of which can come to awareness in the early days of self-exploration. Yet, with wisdom, openness, insight, gentleness, awareness, understanding, care, compassion, empathy and love, profound depths of healing and integration of the psychological-historical shadow can occur. If we gift this to ourselves, and then encourage others to gift the same to themselves, we can transform a world that mirrors the unintegrated and wounded ego into one that reflects a healed and integrated ego and an Authentic Self: Imagine what kind of world we would live in that mirrored the expression of nearly eight billion people centered in their Sovereign Self.

ego/Self Prelude

Consider for a moment the True Self as a King or Queen returning to reclaim the throne. Imagine the many shadow defenses they will encounter along the corridors that lead to the throne room, where they will ultimately meet the wounded and unintegrated ego.

> Here, the Fairytale of 'ego & Self' unfolds:
>
> Ego has realized that Self is returning to reclaim its throne, and in fear and panic frantically barricades the throne room door. Self arrives and knocks on the door requesting that ego relinquish the throne and allow it to enter. A defensive ego refuses to open the door and prepares to take up arms ready to protect its position, for It will do anything to remain enthroned and conveys this to Self through the closed door. Ego tries to intimidate Self into submission in the hope that Self will scurry back to its place of exile.
>
> However, Self rides out the storm that has been whipped up by ego who feels powerless in the full presence of Self and further panics: *What will become of it if Self succeeds in reclaiming the throne?* it wonders. Ego fears it will die. It can see no other outcome and is too afraid to surrender. It does not know what to do and resolutely digs in its heels refusing to open the door. Ego and Self have reached an impasse. Weeks and months pass by with Self ever-present and ego locked in the throne room with no resources to maintain its power and becoming weaker by the day. Ego resolves to die on the throne for surrendering to Self will surely result in the same outcome. Ego prepares for the end - that is until Self throws it a lifeline.

Self begins to speak to ego with great tenderness and the greatest respect. Ego is struck by the compassion and love in Self's voice, believing it to be the kindest it has ever heard. Ego begins to feel very weary and overwhelmed by the exhaustion of a lifetime. It finds itself pouring out its fears to Self who listens with great care and empathy. Ego feels an inexplicable sense of trust in Self, as each of its fears are validated. It begins to consider the possibility of opening the throne room door but, once again, is overcome with fear of the consequences. As much as it wants to trust, for it is so tired, ego is afraid believing that Self will betray it. Ego shares these fears with Self who with such gentleness and compassion offers a written promise that will be sealed in gold stating that ego's life will be safe and its life would be a blessed one from the moment it opened the throne room door. Self slides the document under the still closed door for ego to consider.

Ego reads it, and then notices a separate letter attached that is tied with a golden thread which it opens: It reads:

My dear, dear Ego, I am so grateful for finally having the opportunity to thank you for saving my life. I recognize that without you I would not be here, I would not be alive. You were there when I most needed protecting, and even though I have been in exile for all these years you ensured that no harm would come my way. You have held on to my kingdom and many battles you have endured on my behalf. I know you are battered and bruised, scarred and weary yet you never deserted me. This undertaking has been a great burden for you and took tremendous courage and strength. How can I ever repay you? What price can be placed on a precious life?

You have served me so very well. You have always been, and will always remain, my hero and I know that everything you have ever done was ultimately to protect me. I am humbled in your presence for I know that you have suffered greatly in my name. I see the pain and hurt you have endured, and I see that your heart has been broken. I see the anger and rage you have felt and received. I see the loss you have borne and the loneliness you have experienced. I see how you stood in the line of fire for me when the first perceived threat to my life occurred many moons ago, and how you have repeatedly done so ever since. All that you have withstood has been to preserve and ensure my existence. You have been the most loyal of friends who has never abandoned me. You bear the many scars of the trials and ordeals of this life.

My beloved Ego, I have been asleep. For many, many years I was lost in exile. One day, not so long ago, I heard the most pitiful cry of anguish. I heard a voice scream out in the still of the night, crying "Help me God, set me free as I can no longer live like this. I am so lonely and in so much pain, and I am so tired. Release me from this suffering." That anguished cry awakened me and it was as if I were resurrected. I felt my life force return as I heard that haunted cry and it pierced the very core of my heart. Every cell of my being heard it and I recognized that voice as your own. In that moment, I knew that it was now my turn to save you, my dear and loyal Ego.

Ego, I Am returning as the ruler of my kingdom. I Am as new. Even though alone, I have been protected for all of these years, and I am unscarred and my heart is whole and unbroken.

Dear, dear Ego, would you do me the great honor of being the one I turn to for advice? Let us once more be friends. I have no need of a wounded ego but great need of a healthy one. You no longer need to be lonely, for I am here as your friend. First, you must rest and heal. Would you trust me to guide you to the people and situations that can help you to do this, as well as learn to play, and experience joy and love? Will you rest? I have prepared new rooms for you to live in and a beautiful garden of peace and serenity. What say you, Ego?

Ego fell to the floor heaving with sobs and said to Self "Yes, how very great has been this burden and yet not a burden, but a sacred duty." Ego spoke of the wrong it had done in Self's name; of those it had hurt and how it had hurt itself. Ego hung its head in shame afraid that by telling the truth of its misdemeanors, Self would abandon it.
There was a moment's pause and then Self spoke to Ego in the most compassionate voice saying:

"My dear, dear Ego, I love you unconditionally and deeply understand all you have shared. Can you forgive yourself? Can you recognize that what you did to others was only a result of what had been done to you, and even though this does not justify your actions, it does not make you unworthy."

Ego replied, "Even if I could forgive myself how will those who I have harmed forgive me? Without their forgiveness how can I truly heal and be free?"

Self replied: "Dearest Ego, you cannot know the karma of those who have crossed your path. Perhaps you were a catalyst or a teacher. You may have brought an experience into another's life to support them to redress past misdemeanors. There is so much that we do not know in this realm, why punish yourself? If you stole from someone, now give to someone, or to many: You may give of your time or your resources. If you abused someone, help those who have been abused. If you have killed someone, help others to live. Redress the balance of the actions you regret: For example, where there is fear bring unconditional love.

"Know this Ego, ALL IS FORGIVEN—ALL IS FORGIVEABLE. You need only to deeply understand your actions to be able to forgive yourself and so redress past misdeeds and be free. This is something you can do every day: Let it be a joy to do so."

Ego stood up and with great courage and a shaky hand unlocked and opened the throne room door: Their hearts met before their eyes, and in unison they both stated, "I have missed you friend." From that moment a harmonious, positive, pure and true partnership began. Self took its place upon the throne as ruler of its kingdom, with Ego, now fully healed, a most positive and trusted advisor at its side.

Remember that before we can fully embody the True Self it is the ego that helps us through the toughest of times. When we live as our True Self we no longer react, instead we *respond* from the heart, from our authentic Self and as a result our lives transform. Ultimately, when healing and integrating the ego we need to first acknowledge and validate its role. The ego deserves to be honored and respected no matter what has gone before for it very likely saved our life when it first emerged in early childhood; loyally remaining with us until we were able to reclaim the throne.

Like any parent, the ego was doing the best it could at the time. Recognize that the unintegrated 'negative' ego needs to heal and retire. The positive and integrated ego however, is a wonderful companion to accompany the True Self on the journey of the Soul.

Conscious Evolution

Teaching Two - The Twenty-One Arrows:
A Map for Evolving Consciousness
The Seven Dark, Seven Light
& Seven Rainbow Arrows

Among the First Nations Peoples' Medicine Teachings is a powerful oral wisdom lore known as *The Seven Dark, Seven Light and Seven Rainbow Arrows.* This profoundly deep and revelatory indigenous philosophy lends itself perfectly to our current times as a *map for evolving consciousness.* All twenty-one arrows represent the psycho-spiritual realms within us and serve as a healing tool, oracle, guide, counsellor and friend: Each individual arrow can support us to navigate the trajectorial path of Self-awareness, Self-awakening, Self-integration, Self-realisation, and Self-actualisation.

THE SEVEN DARK, SEVEN LIGHT, & SEVEN RAINBOW ARROWS

The Seven Dark Arrows:

Attachment
Dependency
Judgment
Comparison
Expectation
The Wounded/Needy Child Syndrome
Self-Importance

The Seven Light Arrows:

Self-Awareness
Self-Appreciation
Self-Acceptance
Self-Pleasure (Joyful BEing)
Self-Love
Self-Actualization
Impeccability (In thought/word/action/deed)

The Seven Rainbow Arrows:

Illumination
Introspection
Trust and Innocence
Wisdom
Open Heart-to-Heart Communication
Balance of Male and Female Energies
Abundance and Prosperity

The First Nations People state that for every Dark Arrow consciously broken, we automatically receive a Light Arrow to integrate into our being; and, for every Light Arrow integrated, we are gifted the opportunity to assimilate and harmonize with the teaching and promise of a Rainbow Arrow.

RECLAIMING AND EMBODYING THE TRUE SELF

Fifteen years ago, when I was in the deepest curve of my own psychological healing and reset, I came across the First Nations' Peoples' Wisdom Teaching: *'The Seven Dark, Seven Light, and Seven Rainbow Arrows'*. As I began to connect with these, a deeper level of opening and healing started to occur within me. The Arrows became one of the primary healing modalities I utilised to navigate my way through my own psychological inner-terrain.

In 2009, I began to research the arrows far and wide but could find no extensively written account of the deeper and broader meaning of them. As far as I could discover at that time, the only reference was a succinctly associated *trait* or *quality* ascribed to each arrow. I felt that this unique sacred lore of healing and awakening merited a broader written perspective in the context of psycho-spiritual healing, integration and awakening. So, I began to deeply contemplate each arrow and transcribe the teaching I felt *it* wanted to share in regard to the psycho-spiritual landscape of an individual in these modern times.

Some of the information presented is accompanied by searching questions that the reader might wish to ask themselves. This is mostly the case with the Dark Arrows, although some of the Light Arrows present in this way as well. The remaining Light Arrows, and all of the Rainbow Arrows, follow a different path of Self-enquiry.

THE SEVEN DARK ARROWS

The First Dark Arrow Is Attachment

1. To whom or what are you attached?
2. Where in your body is your attention most drawn when you feel into the experience of attachment?
3. Staying with your felt sense (not your mind) can you feel into the need behind the attachment?
4. What do you need in order to no longer be attached?
5. How might you, another, or life, meet that need?

The spiritual lesson of attachment is — non-attachment.

A sacred mantra for attachment could be: *Even though a part of me can become caught in attachment, I deeply and completely unconditionally love and accept myself.*

The Second Dark Arrow Is Dependency

1. Upon whom or what are you dependent?
2. Where in your body do you experience the feeling of dependency?
3. Staying with your felt sense (not your mind) can you feel into the need behind the dependency?
4. What do you need in order to no longer feel dependent?
5. How might you, another, or life, meet that need?

The spiritual lessons of dependency are — independence, interdependence, and self-love.

A sacred mantra for dependency could be: *Even though a part of me can feel dependent, I deeply and completely unconditionally love and accept myself.*

The Third Dark Arrow Is Judgment

1. How aware are you of the energy of judgment in your life?
2. How much do you feel you self-judge?
3. How aware are you of how you may judge others?
4. How often do you feel judged by others?

Recognize that when you judge others, or experience yourself as being judged, this reveals how you also judge yourself. If you were not self-judging, you would not perceive yourself as being judged and would not judge others. Instead you would understand that when another is judging you, they are projecting their own psychological wounding.

On a scale from 1 to 10 (with 10 holding the strongest charge), how often would you say you judge yourself or others? Be honest with yourself.

5. Set an intent to spend a day self-observing and make notes of how often a judgment arises within you about yourself or another. Take note each time you catch yourself in judgment, and at the end of the day assess how frequently this has occurred.
6. Transform those judgments about yourself or another by thinking, stating or focusing on a positive quality about yourself or the other.
7. What is it you feel you need in order not to judge?
8. How might you, another, or life, meet that need?

The spiritual lessons of judgment are — unconditional positive regard, self-acceptance, and unconditional love.

A sacred mantra for judgment could be: *Even though a part of me does not feel good enough, I deeply and completely unconditionally love and accept myself.*

The Fourth Dark Arrow Is Comparison

1. How aware are you of the energy of comparison in your life?
2. How often do you compare yourself with others?
3. How often do you compare people with each other?
4. How often do you feel that other people are comparing you?

Recognize that when you experience yourself as being compared, or you compare others, this reveals how you compare yourself. If you did not compare yourself, you would not perceive yourself as being compared or compare others. Instead, you would realise that another is projecting their own psychological wounding onto you and your response would be one of understanding. When another compares you, it is because there is a deep need within them that is not being met. Therefore, their comparison is not about you but themselves.

On a scale from 1 to 10 (with 10 holding the strongest charge), how often would you say you compare yourself or others? Be honest with yourself.

5. Set an intent in the days that follow to catch each moment you find yourself comparing. Transform those comparisons by choosing to think, state, feel, or focus on something good and positive about yourself or another.
6. What is it you feel you need in order to not compare?
7. How might you, another, or life, meet that need?

The spiritual lessons of comparison are—unconditional self-love, self-validation, and self-acceptance.

A sacred mantra for comparison could be: *Even though a part of me can become caught in comparison, I deeply, completely and unconditionally love and accept myself.*

The Fifth Dark Arrow Is Expectation

1. How aware are you of the experience of expectation in your life?
2. How often do you expect from yourself, others, or life itself?
3. How often do you feel the weight of expectations of others towards you? Recognize that when you experience others as having expectations of you, or you have expectations of others, this reveals how you have expectations of yourself. The expectations of others is but a reflection of the expectations they have of themselves, and how they are not yet able to meet the needs behind their own expectations.
4. On a scale from 1 to 10 (with 10 holding the strongest charge), how often would you say you have expectations of yourself or others? Be honest with yourself.
5. Set an intent to spend a day self-observing, and make a note of how often expectation arises in relation to yourself or others. Take note each time you catch yourself putting an expectation on yourself or someone else. At the end of the day assess how frequently this has occurred.
6. Try to feel the need behind your own expectation.
7. What need is not being met?
8. What is it that you need in order to get that need met?
9. Set an intent to try to meet that need yourself, or to consciously reach out to another/others expressing what you need and if they are willing to support you to meet it.

The spiritual lessons of *expectation* are - Self-Love, Self-nurture, Self-acceptance, non-attachment, trust, and surrender.

A sacred mantra for *expectation* could be: *Even though a part of me can become caught in expectation, I deeply and completely unconditionally love and accept myself.*

The Sixth Dark Arrow Is the Wounded Inner/Needy Child Syndrome

1. How aware are you of the presence of the wounded inner-child within you?
2. In what way do you experience your wounded inner-child?
3. On a scale of 1 - 10 (10 holding the strongest charge), how often would you say you experience yourself as 'needy'? Be honest with yourself.
4. Set an intent to spend a day self-observing, and make notes of how often you are aware of your inner-wounded/needy child. Write down each moment of realisation, no matter how fleeting or seemingly insignificant. At the end of the day, assess how often your inner-wounded/needy child has been present.
5. Set an intent over the days to follow to catch and record each moment you experience your needy inner-child.
6. Try to feel what is behind his/her emotions and reactions: Is she/he feeling fearful, unsafe, hurt, sad, or angry? Does he/she need to feel secure, seen, heard, held, validated and acknowledged?
7. What need is not being met?
8. How can the adult you (inner-parent) meet that need?
9. How might others support your wounded/needy inner-child?
10. Set an intent to try to meet those needs yourself, or to consciously reach out to another/others with whom your inner-wounded/needy child feels safe, who may wish to support you. Openly express what you need.
11. Recognize that when you experience another as needy this is likely to stem from the unmet needs of their own wounded/needy inner-child. Such an experience can also act as a mirror, as a reminder, that your own wounded inner-child is in need of love and healing. Seek to respond with compassion and understanding,

and remain mindful in that moment that you are not addressing an adult but the wounded inner-child within yourself, or the other.

The spiritual lessons of the wounded/needy inner-child are - trust, inner authority, self-love, compassion, empathy, deep understanding, and forgiveness.

A sacred mantra for the wounded/needy inner-child could be: *Even though I am aware of the wounded and needy child within me, I deeply, completely and unconditionally love and accept myself.*

The Seventh Dark Arrow Is Self-Importance

1. To what degree are you aware of the dark arrow of self-importance? How alive is that energy within you?
2. Take some time to write, sketch, or paint what you become aware of when observing yourself in the mode of self-importance.
3. On a scale from 1 to 10 (with 10 holding the strongest charge), how often do you experience yourself caught in self-importance? Be honest with yourself.
4. Set an intent to spend a day self-observing, and make notes of how often you become aware of your own experiences of self-importance. Each time this occurs, record the situation and your reaction of self-importance. At the end of the day, assess how frequently you have experienced yourself in this mode. Write down how you feel in those moments of realization.
5. Try to gain a sense of the needs behind your experiences.
6. Set out to identify the need within you that is not being met and what original (historical) need was not met. What do you need in order to meet that now? Go with your first response, and without censoring write whatever comes.
7. How can you begin to meet that need yourself?

8. How might another, or others, or life, meet that need with you in a healthy way?
9. Reach out to those you trust who are consciously aware and express what you need. Ask if they would be willing to support you to meet that.
10. The act of self-importance originates from traumatic experiences or unmet needs in childhood, as well as from karmic and ancestral influences.

The spiritual lessons of self-importance are – humility; the healing and integration of the unintegrated ego; and evolving from power-over (ego defence) to empowered (Self-integration).

A sacred mantra for self-importance could be: *Even though I am aware of a part of me that becomes caught in self-importance, I deeply, completely and unconditionally love and accept myself.*

THE SEVEN LIGHT ARROWS

The First Light Arrow Is Self-Awareness

From a psycho-spiritual perspective, it has long been theorized that there are differing levels of consciousness. This theory entered the mainstream when American psychologist and philosopher William James, who was trained as a physician, postulated in 'The Principles of Psychology' (1890) that *there existed a physical, mental, and spiritual self and ego.* In approximately 1905, the Austrian Psycho-Analyst, Sigmund Freud, presupposed *an unconscious, preconscious, and conscious mind.*

Being psychologically self-aware requires a greater degree of psychological insight and a deeper understanding of the mechanisms and workings of the unconscious, conscious and superconscious minds. In psychological language, the term *ego* equates to the *psychological shadow, unintegrated personality, and historically wounded inner-child* (*child of history*). We are also aware of the constant presence of Soul, Spirit, Energy and Creative Force. Our dreams convey important information to be integrated during our waking hours. Self-awareness facilitates the awakening or deepening of our connection to the spiritual dimensions within ourselves, which results in a greater capacity for perception, cognition, intuition, creativity, visioning, and gnosis. Psychological self-awareness also invites us to re-connect to, embrace, and embody *the golden child* (soul child) that lives within each of us.

The First Light Arrow is Self-Awareness. We could say that Self-awareness covers a broad spectrum of past events, our current lives, and future hopes. Self-awareness requires a commitment to self-exploration and our capacity to self-analyse at a deeper psychological level; therefore (re)connecting more fully at a spiritual level. It is also facilitated through non-judgemental self-reflection and self-directed and autonomous thinking.

Self-awareness requires that we develop an inner-dialogue between the wisest part of ourselves - the *Authentic Self* - (reference

'The ego/Self Fairytale') - and the historically-psychologically inner wounded 'self' - the *'adapted self'*. It invites us to turn our attention inward. By becoming more self-aware, we become more familiar with our psychological edges; our propensity towards *reaction* (wounded self), rather than *response* (healed self). We are more aware of our psychological story, and how the 'myths' from our past (karmic and ancestral) can impact us in the here and now. We are able to adequately self-evaluate, self-reflect and self-guide as we come to more fully know and trust ourselves.

Being Self-aware enables us to monitor and observe our thoughts, actions, beliefs, perceptions, emotions, sensations and impulses. We are continually assessing our motives, drives and intentions. We listen deeply and are guided by our felt sense. We are more able to effect necessary and evolutionary changes in our lives. Our emotional and mental landscapes become expanded and more fertile. Self-awareness enables us to reprogram the unconscious mind, re-inform the conscious mind, and (re)connect to the superconscious mind.

Self-awareness is supported by our ability to self-observe. We are curious about ourselves, and the reasons for the patterns and themes in our lives.

When embraced as a daily practice, Self-awareness becomes instinctual: This can be illustrated by the analogy of driving a car: When we first take a driving lesson, we need to become familiar with all the fundamental and basic mechanisms involved in how to make it move. Yet, in a very short while, the process becomes automatic, natural even, and we no longer need to think about the step-by-step mechanics of driving, which has become an effortless automation.

Becoming Self-aware marks a psycho-spiritual watershed on our journey of awakening: Its effect is akin to a veil being lifted, a light turned on in the dark, a once misty screen having become clear.

A sacred mantra for Self-awareness could be: I choose to manifest my greatest potential and therefore I commit more fully to becoming Self-aware. And, I deeply, completely and unconditionally love and accept myself.

The Second Light Arrow Is Self-Acceptance

The Second Light Arrow of Self-Acceptance invites us to break the dark arrows of *comparison* and *judgment*.

1. Find a quiet moment and assess where along the scale of self-acceptance you feel you are — 1 being the least self-accepting and 10 the most. Trust your initial response.
2. What would it feel like to unconditionally accept yourself, even your psychological shadow aspects that can make you feel uncomfortable?
3. Set aside some time to identify all you find difficult to accept about yourself.
4. Recognize that when you stop judging and comparing yourself, you immediately experience a more positive sense of who you really are.
5. When asking the question "Who am I?", it is usually the adapted self (unintegrated ego) that replies, giving an entirely false account. The enquiry into *Who am I* is a question for the Self. To more fully embody the Self (see ego/Self Fairytale), we need to embrace all the Light Arrows.
6. True self-acceptance connects you to your Authentic (True) Self.
7. Find some time to contemplate what you feel *is* authentic about you. What would you really wish for people to know? Write those qualities down and keep them close to hand.
8. Set aside some time to write a story about your 'True Self'. This is a powerful way to get to know more about *who you really are* beyond any psychological/historical wounding; and can help you to anchor *the more than you are* into your unconscious and conscious mind. Allow your imagination (the soul in action) to flow uncensored. *Who are you deep in your heart and soul?*

9. For the next seven days, seek to know what it is that you find difficult to accept about yourself, and what shadow aspects you may yearn to let go. Write it all down and at the end of the week, or when you feel ready, consciously and mindfully burn the list blessing each 'concern' on its way as you watch it dissolve in the flames. This process can be done in rounds, and so it may take several weeks or months for surface layers to dissipate and give way to deeper layers of shadow (wounding) to rise to the surface of your awareness. As you commit each 'issue' to the flames, see it as being transmuted into LIGHT.
10. Believe in your innate goodness.
11. Treat yourself with loving kindness.
12. Love yourself unconditionally.
13. Trust your wise and loving heart.

A sacred mantra for Self-acceptance could be: *I deeply, completely and unconditionally love and accept myself.*

The Third Light Arrow Is **Self-Appreciation**

1. Find a quiet moment and assess where along the scale you are in terms of Self-Appreciation—with 1 being the least Self-appreciating and 10 being the most. Where on that scale are you? Trust your initial response.
2. What would it feel like to unconditionally appreciate yourself?
3. Recognize that by no longer judging and comparing yourself, you immediately hold the Light Arrow of Self-appreciation in your hands.
4. Take some moments to contemplate what you really appreciate about YOU. Write those qualities down and keep them close to hand. Every time you pick up the dark arrows of *judgment* and *comparison,* take a look at the qualities you have written down and visualize discarding those

dark arrows and replacing them with the Light Arrows of *self-acceptance* and *self-appreciation*.
5. Each day, appreciate something about yourself. State what this is aloud. Look at your reflection in a mirror and express what it is that you do appreciate about yourself and why.
6. When you appreciate something in another, turn that thought around, and appreciate the same quality within you. If you did not possess that quality, you would not be able to recognize it in another.

A sacred mantra for Self-appreciation could be: *I now choose to appreciate myself more. I deeply and completely unconditionally love and accept myself.*

The Fourth Light Arrow Is Self-Pleasure

The Fourth Light Arrow focuses on Self-pleasure and how this can connect us to both our earthly and divine selves. The Light Arrow of Self-pleasure refers to anything the *whole and integrated* Self experiences as *pleasurable*. When we experience Self-pleasure from this state of BEing, we are more fully aligned and connected with the psycho-spiritual multi-levels within ourselves: *From ego to I, and personality to soul.*

The experience of pure Self-pleasure is the birthright of every human being: Most happy young children are in this mode much of the time. It re-connects us to *innocence*, which leads to greater Self-trust and Self-fulfilment.

The phenomenon of Self-pleasure has become lost to the world and reduced to a distorted (mis)representation of what is truly at its core. Every human being has a basic need for pleasure. This fundamental necessity is a prerequisite for overall wellbeing and living a balanced and fulfilled life. Self-pleasure takes many forms, all of which are expressions of pure unadulterated love and joy – joyfully loving ourselves.

Sacred sexuality with the Self (another form of Self-pleasure) can open us to transcendent states of consciousness and higher dimensional experiences. It purifies and heals. Yet, this form of Self-pleasure may often instil a sense of shame or guilt within the unintegrated and unhealed wounded self. By allowing ourselves to openly acknowledge such feelings, we can initiate the process of healing and move closer to the experience of Self-Love; a prerequisite for the expression of sacred sexuality with Self. Sexual Self-pleasure, when encapsulated in the physical, emotional and mental energy of purity, is a gateway to the sublime – and can lead us into a mystical and momentary experience of Self-transcendence.

A sacred mantra for Self-pleasure could be: *I choose to consciously engage in sacred, joyful and loving experiences of Self-pleasure. I deeply, completely and unconditionally love and accept myself.*

The Fifth Light Arrow Is Self-Love

1. Where along the scale of Self-love do you feel you are, with 1 being the least self-loving and 10 the most? Trust your initial response.
2. What would it feel like to unconditionally love yourself?
3. Recognize that by releasing the dark arrows of *self-judgment* and *self-comparison,* you immediately pick up the Light Arrow of *Self-love.*
4. Take some moments to contemplate what it is that you *do* love about yourself. Write those qualities down and keep them close to you. Every time you pick up the dark arrows of *judgment* and *comparison*, take a look at the qualities you have written down and visualize discarding those arrows and gifting yourself with the Light Arrows of *Self-love, Self-acceptance*, and *Self-appreciation*.
5. Each day, find something *more* to love about yourself. State out loud what this is and then look at yourself in a mirror and repeat the statement again.

6. Set an intent to love yourself unconditionally.
7. When you find yourself loving a quality in another, turn that around and love that same quality in yourself. You would not be able to recognize the quality in the other were it not already within you.

A sacred mantra for Self-love could be: *I choose to love myself more. I deeply, completely and unconditionally love and accept myself.*

The Sixth Light Arrow Is Self-Actualization

In his article, 'A Theory of Human Motivation' (1943), the psychologist Abraham Maslow presented a psychological explanation for Self-actualization:

Self-actualization refers to the desire for self-fulfilment, namely, to the tendency for the individual to become actualized in what he or she is potentially. Self-actualization might be described as the desire to become more and more what one is, to become everything that one is capable of becoming.

Maslow identified some of the key characteristics to be found in Self-actualized people:

Acceptance and Realism: Self-actualized people have realistic perceptions of themselves, others, and the world around them.

Problem-Centring: Self-actualized individuals are concerned with solving problems outside of themselves, including helping others and finding solutions to problems in the external world. These people are often motivated by a sense of personal responsibility and ethics.

Spontaneity: Self-actualized people are spontaneous in their internal thoughts and outward behaviour. While they can conform to rules and social expectations, they also tend to be open and unconventional.

Autonomy and Solitude: A further characteristic of self-actualized people is the need for independence and privacy. While they enjoy the company of others, these individuals need time to focus on developing their own individual potential.

Continued Freshness of Appreciation: Self-actualized people tend to view the world with a continual sense of appreciation, wonder, and awe. Even simple experiences are a constant source of inspiration and pleasure.

Peak Experiences: Individuals who are self-actualized often have *peak experiences,* or moments of *intense joy, wonder, awe,* and *ecstasy.* After these experiences, people feel *inspired, strengthened, renewed, or transformed.*

Maslow's description of Self-actualization is a valid model and provides an insightful map for guiding us along the path of our own psychological evolution.

Self-actualization has a higher spiritual octave: Throughout time, mystics and sages have taught that Self-actualization extends far beyond the boundaries of the psychological and physical realms. It also serves as a bridge between the embodied states of *Self-actualisation* and *Self-transcendence*; the latter of which is rarely achieved and hitherto now only by those who have exemplified the most advanced states of awakening - Buddha and Yeshua are just two examples. However, there are many other highly evolved souls who have chosen to incarnate on this Earth, some of whom have been and gone, and yet others who *are* currently here; many of whom are unsung, and unknown to the world.

The spiritual-evolutionary trajectory of the awakened individual is such that it compels one to strive towards the most exalted expression of human *BEing*. To be Self-actualized is to *transcend* the limitations of the unconscious mind and psychological, karmic and ancestral (personal and collective) imprinting and conditioning.

Self-actualization compels us to strive for the highest ideals in regard to becoming a *perfected expression of a soul incarnate in human form*. When we no longer carry the dark arrows and instead hold only the Light, we have attained the state of Self-actualization. At this point, we experience an evolutionary leap in consciousness and align more fully with the Superconscious mind.

A sacred mantra for Self-actualization could be: *I choose to dedicate myself to embodying the state of Self-actualisation and becoming Self Actualised in the world. I deeply and completely unconditionally love and accept myself.*

The Seventh Light Arrow Is Impeccability

The Seventh Light Arrow requires us to cultivate *impeccability* in word, thought, action and deed. Impeccability is a mode of *BEing* in which our conduct, presence and actions are expressed to the highest evolved degree. This Arrow bestows pristine clarity. It calls for purity in the arena of relationships, including our relationship with ourselves, others, and the world. Impeccable Self-conduct is the core focus of this Light Arrow. When we are holding it in our hands, we are experiencing ourselves, and are experienced by others, as highly-refined, deeply sincere, fully responsible and accountable, and profoundly aware. The focus of one who carries the Seventh Light Arrow is on the full embodiment of the Authentic Self.

Impeccability differs from perfection in that the quest for the latter can cause one to suffer, whereas the former gifts us the ongoing experience of ease of expression and accompanying joy when implementing and upholding the highest ideals and values. Perfectionism, on the other hand, can create a lack of fulfilment or satisfaction. If our quest for impeccability causes suffering to ourselves or anyone else, then we are caught in the shadow of perfectionism.

This arrow requires us to scrutinize our conduct under a magnifying glass in order to reveal where we may further refine the intent behind all that we do and say. Impeccability requires absolute commitment to attaining the purest states of physical, emotional, mental, psychological, energetic and psychic being, and calls on us to live from pure clarity and intent. It invites us to live transparently, and to be scrupulously honest, to honour our word and our commitments; and to *walk our impeccable* talk.

One who lives from impeccability no longer needs to carry the Seven Dark Arrows of *attachment, dependency, judgment, comparison, expectation, the wounded/needy child syndrome,* and *self-importance*. Instead, they are equipped with the Seven Light Arrows of *self-awareness, self-acceptance, self-appreciation, self-pleasure, self-love, self-actualization,* and *impeccability,* and are ready to take the next step on their journey of conscious evolution – integrating and embodying the Seven Rainbow Arrows.

When we carry the Seventh Light Arrow of Impeccability, we have attained an elevated state that exerts a beneficial influence on all we encounter. When we live from impeccability, we experience ourselves, and are experienced by others, as impeccable in all that we say or do. The Seventh Light Arrow can be likened to a tuning fork in that the tone it emits is one of the highest and purest frequencies, which can support others to realign with a higher vibration and higher level of consciousness.

A sacred mantra for impeccability could be: *I choose to cultivate and embody impeccability in every word, thought, action, and deed. I deeply and completely unconditionally love and accept myself.*

THE SEVEN RAINBOW ARROWS

We shall now begin our exploration of the Seven Rainbow Arrows.

The First Rainbow Arrow Is Illumination

The Consciousness of the *true* Mystic is one of Illumination. Such a physically embodied soul has a rare and unique experience of The Absolute. The Illumined Self is regularly subjected to transcendental states, including those described as 'peak' experiences. Illumination is an exalted condition in which one is steeped in rapture and bliss, and is in *LOVE* with the totality of Creation and Life.

Transcendent qualities accompany the illumined state. Those who exemplify this have often plumbed the depths of the unconscious – of both the Self and the Collective - and are Messengers for the deepest wisdom and highest truths. They are at one with the material world and otherworldly realities. To be illuminated is to pulse with LIGHT and transmit the very essence of LOVE.

The Second Rainbow Arrow Is Introspection

Introspection is the gateway to Self-awareness and Self-realization. The pioneering and visionary Carl Gustav Jung, wrote:

Your vision will become clear only when you look into your heart . . . Who looks outside, dreams. Who looks inside, awakens.

To *look inside* is to potentially open Pandora's Box. For, as we lift its lid, all that is contained within it that has been repressed, split-off or denied will rise to the surface for healing and integration. Many are afraid to *look inside* for fear of what they may encounter, of what may have been buried deep within the unconscious a long time ago. Ultimately however, under the auspices of the soul and divine timing, we will feel called and compelled to *look inside*, knowing/gno-ing (gnosis) that the only way we can cut the ties that bind us to unfulfilled and inauthentic being is by doing so.

How can we best utilise the Second Rainbow Arrow of Introspection?

First, we need to set aside the necessary time to explore the psychological dimensions of ourselves. Working one-to-one with a highly-reputable practitioner who is professionally skilled at holding psycho-spiritual (psychological and spiritual) space, and is able to listen deeply, no matter what stories present, and who knows/gno's (gnosis) how to respond appropriately and wisely, can support us to heal self-sabotaging patterns and lift the shadow of a life lived under the dictum of inner-wounding. Instead, we begin to embrace a new way of *living;* a new experience of feeling ALIVE; a new mode of BEing that is liberating and *life-serving.*

Secondly, a willingness to examine the origins of our thoughts, emotions, motivations, desires, drives, decisions, words and actions, helps us to heal and transform our lives. Inner-peace is the promise of the Second Rainbow Arrow of Introspection. Take hold of it and dare to *look inside* 'Pandoras Box', for, in doing so, you will discover the greatest treasure of all - your True and Authentic Self.

The Third Rainbow Arrow Is Trust and Innocence

Trust is to be found at the core of all meaningful and profoundly enduring relationships. It is the very heartbeat of the *true* relationship we can have with ourselves. Without trust we cannot bond and are therefore unable to experience the full extent of *right relationship* with ourselves or others.

The roots of mistrust can be traced back to infancy - at least in this lifetime. Infancy renders us entirely vulnerable and dependent on others. The degree to which we trust originates from the quality of loving and mindful care that was given to us by primary caregivers. As children, when we are taught by example that it is safe to trust we grow into adulthood feeling secure in the world. Yet, if our primary caregivers were emotionally or physically absent, and/or were abusive, unreliable, dishonest, contradictory or rejecting, the wound of mistrust can deeply imprint into the unconscious mind where it remains festering until it is healed.

Where trust has been broken, a schism occurs within the emotional and mental bodies and the psychological symptoms of distrust are the result. We may then view the world hostile, an unpredictable and unsafe place, and we ourselves may be experienced by others as similar.

> Here are some signs that may suggest you have trust issues: fear of intimacy, suspicion, anxiety in many forms including during physical intimacy, impotence, inability to orgasm or inability to orgasm when sexually intimate with a partner, panic attacks, irrational fear and terror, agoraphobia, claustrophobia, phobias in general, repeated patterns of relationship breakdown (romance or friends), and attracting dishonesty, betrayal, or deception.

There is a difference between fulfilment and security. The need for the latter can supersede the former in that we can run our lives on fear and make decisions based on our primary need for security at all costs.

Security is *the known,* and yet it can be restrictive; a self-imposed prison in which we feel the safest. When we are able to trust, we more readily embrace the *unknown,* and its potential challenges are viewed and experienced as opportunities that facilitate growth and set us on adventures that can lead to profound fulfilment.

The invitation of the Third Rainbow Arrow of Trust and Innocence is to *return to innocence.* If betrayal, deception, or the loss of innocence, (in any given relationship or scenario), are recurring themes in your life, it is quite possible that you are unconsciously *re-creating your history to do now what you could not do back then* - in terms of empowering and ultimately freeing yourself from the chains of the past.

Unless we consciously seek to heal issues of trust, we will continue to attract related patterns as *opportunities* (for this is what they are) for healing, integration and liberation. You *can* learn to trust again ... and you *can* reclaim lost innocence: The 15th Century Philosopher Paracelsus spoke of this when he shared that *there is small piece of heaven inside each one of us that remains whole and unbroken*. Find that heaven within and, slowly but surely, it will expand until, once again, it fills your entire being.

The degree to which you can trust is the gauge by which you can measure how present trust or mistrust are in the overall experience of your life. Empathy, understanding, compassion and unconditional love are the potent medicines that are necessary to heal the wounds of mistrust and support the reclaiming of lost innocence.

The Fourth Rainbow Arrow Is Wisdom

The Fourth Rainbow Arrow teaches that true wisdom is not rationale, intellect, mental prowess, or academic brilliance. The wisdom this Arrow primarily points to is its truest expression - the type that is borne of gnosis – *knowing, yet not knowing how we know, we just know*. It speaks of perception and intuition; the whispers of Spirit; the equilibrium of heart and mind under the direction of the soul. It calls our attention to the promptings of the 'sixth sense'; of a higher intelligence, the *still small voice within* that bestows wise counsel; the lens through which the visionary Self peers; wisdom in the form of premonition; unshakeable conviction.

The world's insatiable thirst for knowledge has prioritised the intellect and its *need to know*, which is celebrated and rewarded in modern culture at the cost of the equal revering of true wisdom. Generally, people are inclined to hide their true feelings due to cultural, familiar, and religious conditioning: Yet true wisdom is the language of the heart. To carry the Fourth Rainbow Arrow of Wisdom requires actively working with the Seven Dark Arrows.

Adapting our authentic truth, hiding our real feelings, silencing our inner-voice, and/or saying or doing what we feel is necessary in order to please or placate, all carry a high price in terms of our physical, emotional, mental, psychological, and energetic wellbeing. An equal balance of *knowledge* and *wisdom, knowing* and *gnosis,* are the ideal and healthy expression of this Arrow. A person with an overly-developed intellect who places too much emphasis on knowledge at the expense of wisdom will never be truly wise.

Throughout history, the good, the great, and the honest and true, have all been recognized by the virtues of their heart and the keenly felt presence of their soul. Knowledge for the sake of knowledge disconnects us from the heart. In mainstream society, the fevered and almost exclusive pursuit of knowledge has diminished and disregarded the natural phenomenon that is pure wisdom. The true seat of wisdom *is* the heart, which holds the greatest knowledge of all – and it is only this type of wisdom and knowing that can ultimately transform the world.

The Fifth Rainbow Arrow Is Open Heart-to-Heart Communication

In the 1950s, the pioneering psychologist Carl Rogers, made the following statement in regard to communication: *Love, genuineness, and empathy are the three essential elements to constructive communication.*

The Fifth Rainbow Arrows invites us to communicate in ways that are loving and kind. It speaks of Love as being the foundation upon which all communication must be built. Communication can result in the triggering of unconscious memories that may be projected onto others. We need to understand what is behind our *reactions* in any given communication. Unless we have been raised by psychologically balanced and consciously evolved parents and caregivers, it is likely that we have never learned how to effectively and naturally communicate with others. The primary caregivers in our infancy through to adulthood are likely to have been raised under similar conditions, and are therefore merely repeating historical patterns that can go back generations.

The majority of people have rarely experienced heart-to-heart communication. The repressive and dualistic model of the mainstream education system fails us in the respect of an absence of *conscious communication* forming an essential part of its curriculum. However, we live in times where we are able to explore more meaningful ways of communication. The old dysfunctional models serve mostly to polarise people, often into positions of defence or attack. We have only to look at the mainstream media and within the working environments of the wider community to see evidence of this.

We have been raised in a repressive and fear-based society in which honesty often equates to blame, shame, rejection, judgment and attack; and so, dishonesty, disconnection and repression have been unconsciously adopted as principle ways to survive. We have *adapted in order to survive.*

Transpersonal psychotherapy speaks of an *adapted self* and an *Authentic Self*; a subject I explore deeply in 'The ego/Self Fairytale'. In order to survive, the True Self retreats into hiding owing to the incongruency of the environment and the threatening messages it conveys.

In NVC (Nonviolent Communication) there is a model for heartful communicating that consists of the following four-steps:

Observing - Feeling - Needing - Requesting:

- *What am I noticing/observing?*
- *What am I feeling?*
- *What do I need?*

- *What is my request?*
- *What are you noticing/observing?*
- *What are you feeling?*
- *What do you need?*
- *What is your request?*

Such simple communication begins to open the channels of the heart and therefore heart-to-heart communication.

When we engage with these four basic principles, we understand not only our own basic feelings and needs but what may be similar in others. Practiced regularly, these four steps can guide us towards *compassionate communication* and teach us to see, hear, validate, acknowledge, and mindfully express our needs. This form of communication is a pre-requisite for ongoing harmonious relations.

Heart-to-Heart Communication can transform your life as you learn to communicate your feelings, emotions and thoughts in ways that are non-violent and preclude reactions such as naming, blaming, shaming, defending, rejecting, or attacking. The gift of the Fifth Rainbow Arrow of Heart-to-Heart Communication is to help us learn to *respond* through deep understanding, compassion, empathy, and unconditional love. When we are able to embrace this mode of BEing as the norm in our lives, we will have come home to our heart.

The Sixth Rainbow Arrow Is Balancing Male and Female Energies

It is believed that many thousands of years ago, when the soul first incarnated on Earth, that each descended in the form of a single androgynous Being of equal male-female balance. It is also believed that as the soul descended further into matter, and became increasingly attached to the physical plane and sensory pleasures of worldly life, it began to lose the full spectrum of its pure divine connection to SOURCE/GOD.

Instead, it is said that the androgynous incarnate soul began to develop a *separation consciousness*, which resulted in the birth of the ego; and thus, the androgynous form separated into two halves that took on the distinct genders of 'male' and 'female'. Since then, it is proposed that the soul has remained on the earthly wheel of death and rebirth until it is once again reunited androgynously with its 'other half'.

Within the male template is contained the blueprint of the female, and within the female the blueprint of the male. For each incarnation, whatever gender our form takes, and we have lived as both genders in other times, we have been developing dual aspects of male-female expression to the point where the male can embody a greater degree of feminine qualities, and the female, greater degrees of the masculine, in our quest to find the perfect balance of both within one form. Conversely, a soul may incarnate into a male form in order to immerse itself in 'all things masculine' having perhaps just completed a series of feminine lives. The same applies to females, who may also have chosen to develop and fully experience all that pertains to the feminine in a single life, having perhaps just finished a series of masculine incarnations.

Regardless of the soul's agenda for the integration of male and female energies, and irrespective of how much we may personally be polarized into definitive expressions of gender, we still retain an equally balanced male/female template within us, and so will always be drawn to expressing such in its ultimate perfected form. The balancing of male-female energies is a prerequisite for magnetizing healthy and functional relationships, and perhaps even an 'other half' reunion. Humankind has lived through grand sweeping ages where either the matriarch reigned, or the patriarch dominated. Yet the present day calls for *gender fluidity* and disassociation from previous gender categorisations. This new age upon us is one in which gender-fluid autonomy and altruistic sovereignty will reign.

We are entering a new conscious epoch in which gender-fluidity (the perfect male-female balance) transcends outmoded gender identification. It is time to celebrate gender-fluidity as well as initiate a more integrated expression of the 'masculine' and 'feminine'. We are evolving beyond the classic astrological gender interpretations of Mars (masculine) and Venus (feminine), and towards their *higher octaves* of 'Pluto' (Mars), who in this case speaks of *transformation* and *transmutation*; and 'Neptune' (Venus), who speaks of *boundarilessness* and *unconditional love*.

The Sixth Rainbow Arrow of Male-Female balance offers an evolutionary call to embrace a more androgynous mode of being. The boundaries between people, authorities, nations, and gender are seeking to be dissolved. It is time for all to be equal in the eyes of ALL. We can each be empathic and constructive; compassionate and passionate; sensitive and strong; receptive and dynamic; intuitive and rationalistic; still and active; linear and creative. In the embodying of these seemingly (conditioned) male-female polarities, we move closer to the embodiment of our Divine Selves – where the balance of the Divine Feminine and the Divine Masculine comes as natural to us as breathing.

The Seventh Rainbow Arrow Is Abundance and Prosperity

Most people yearn to live an abundant and prosperous life, but what exactly does this mean when holding the Seventh Rainbow Arrow of Abundance and Prosperity? Does it refer to financial wealth? Is it the type of abundance and prosperity that is gained through overwork? Is it an expression of such that robs our time, our heart, or attempts to steal our soul? Is it the kind of abundance and prosperity gained through dishonest means … through greed or betrayal? Is it a level of abundance and prosperity that has been generated through the darker agendas of the human shadow, and not the altruistic benevolence of the human heart? Or, does the Seventh Rainbow Arrow speak of the riches to be found in the depths of the *ensouled heart?* Could it be representing the emotional, mental, psychological, and spiritual wealth to be enjoyed when we are present in such a way to make another's heart sing?

There is an enormous divide in the world between material poverty and wealth, and we may often wonder just how it is that so many are financially rich and yet, by contrast, so many others are materially poor. Some of those who may be deemed by society to be 'poor' can bring the greatest riches to this world. A person may work tirelessly but their heart may shine while doing so. If you were to ask them *why this is,* they might tell you that even though they may lack materially, they feel wealthy beyond measure because they live from their heart and soul. These individuals are a gift to the world.

True abundance and prosperity *are* experiences of the heart and soul, which are always abundant and prosperous. An open heart gives and receives unconditionally, for it is sustained by LOVE. The duality of *rich or poor,* and the polarity of "success" and "failure", needs to be healed in a world that has lost its moral compass. Money is merely energy. We each have something of greatest value to contribute to Life and each other, and if we were all to share our gifts - be those material abundance or the prosperity of Love - the world would thrive in a beautiful experience of true abundance and prosperity, perhaps for the first time in its history.

There is nothing sordid about financial wealth when we are willing to share it with others and to utilize it to help make the world a healthier and more inspired place. What is important from both ends of the spectrum in terms of "rich versus poor", is an open and giving heart ... kindness, goodness and unconditional generosity ... compassion, understanding and love. In an ideal world, we would be able to ask each other for what we need with our dignity remaining intact.

When we leave these mortal bodies, we will not be taking our possessions with us. The spiritual merit of the life we will have just transcended is not measured by our bank balances or savings accounts. The only wealth that registers on the other side of the veil is the legacy of Love we gifted the world while we were in it. The life we have led until we return HOME is measured by all that we did in in the name of LOVE, the degree to which we gave unconditionally from our heart, and how much our presence blessed others with the experience of true abundance and prosperity.

Yet still the merit is not so much about the material support we gave to others, but the motive behind it and the purity of intent in which it was given. How we lived our lives and how our presence touched the soul of the world are the akashic imprints that register within the blueprint of our own soul after we have returned HOME. And if we are to reincarnate into another life on Earth, then those imprints will determine the quality of inner-peace we experience in that next life, irrespective of whether our soul may have chosen a 'materially rich' or 'financially poor' existence.

As long as we are affluent in our hearts and rich in our souls and bestow such wealth upon all we encounter, we will not only be carrying the Seventh Rainbow Arrow but will have mastered it. The Seventh Rainbow Arrows speaks of equality - where *all* are considered equal, and *all* of Gaia's children – species wide – can laugh and play in freedom; where *all living beings* are liberated from suffering, and lack; and where Gaia Herself is honoured for the truly abundant and prosperous Mother that She *Is* to All of Us.

Spiritual Awakening

Teaching Three - The Twelve Phases of Ascension

In March 2009, I was guided to write about the 'Ascension Process' following my own ongoing experience, which began when I was sixteen years old. Just as was/is the case for myself, those who are spiritually and consciously awakening, automatically begin to catalyze a change of vibration as they 'upgrade' and embody a higher frequency within their energetic form.

This evolutionary process can dramatically impact the human physical body, which may change shape; our eyes and skin may change color; the hairline may recede in both male and females and grow finer or thicker; our overall physical appearance may undergo subtle or radical changes, and our voices may alter in their pitch and tone.

Some may gain weight even though they eat sparsely, which allows them to accommodate downloads of incoming energies in order to be able to act as frequency transmitters, while others can substantially lose weight even though they are eating well, as their finely tuned antennae picks up subtle galactic information and messages streaming from our Galaxy and Cosmos.

5th dimensional alignment both interrupts and alters our patterning supporting us to become discerning and empowered in our choices. It can significantly increase our creative expression.

Our capacity to BE LOVE - that is to love unconditionally and Consciously - exponentiates as we come to more fully understand that the most important role we are here to fulfill in the world is to Love. We comprehend just why we are really here on this beautiful Earth and are able to fulfil our Higher Purpose, which at the very least, is to Love and then Love even more.

By becoming the embodiment of Unconditional LOVE, we amplify the Light and raise the frequency of the world.

The ascension process is a psycho-spiritual phenomenon that revolves around twelve 'awakening' phases. Some may move through these in linear and sequential stages, whereas others may experience them non-sequentially and simultaneously. Ultimately, each stage must be integrated within the Self. The twelve phases are based on my own deeply experienced insights along with channelled information, and also include some illuminating additions from Tashira Tachi-ren and Jasmuheen.

The Twelve Phases of Ascension

PHASE ONE

You may experience short or prolonged bouts of debilitating exhaustion. Strong reactions to intense solar and galactic energies can result in random, transitory or intense physical symptoms - (check the list at the end of this section). Mild symptoms can be indicative of nearing the completion of a phase, or might suggest you are about to enter it.

Intense symptoms point to one of two possibilities - a deep and/or rapid purging of ancient/historical stories stored at cellular and soulular level, or a breakthrough in unconscious resistance to the awakening process.

If you are not implementing the necessary changes in your life that any given phase requires, you may find yourself unable to move through the physical symptoms. In this case it would be conducive to seek the support of a reputable psycho-spiritual practitioner/body-energy worker.

PHASE TWO

Phase two is marked by what appears to be mild flu symptoms as well as extreme bouts of tiredness and physical weakness. Muscles ache and energy supply to the limbs feels blocked as the life force is needed elsewhere within the physical-energetic system.

You may wonder if you have conditions such as Fibromyalgia, Adrenal Burnout, or ME, which closely mimic ascension symptoms. In such cases it is wise to get checked over by a GP. Similar symptoms to Phase One remain only these may be more acute.

At times you can feel disoriented. Karma will begin to spontaneously release through the body. You may find yourself experiencing an existential crisis as you deeply contemplate and re-evaluate your life. Nausea and dizziness are common as higher-dimensional frequencies and solar and galactic energies continue to download into the 'Lightbody'.

You may experience a 'spinning' sensation as the emotional and mental bodies and chakra system process the necessary physical-energetic adjustments. Rapid changes begin to occur in all areas of your life. You will have embraced vegetarianism at this stage.

PHASE THREE

Your senses are refining and your perception, intuition and capacity for gnosis become more finely tuned as your physical and energy bodies entrain and align with higher vibrational forces. Intense symptoms remain and exhaustion can be common but will begin to lift for longer periods of time. Physical strength begins to return. Lucid dreams, OBE's and 'psychic' phenomena are more likely to be experienced from this stage onwards. This is the Phase when you begin to master the physical body.

PHASE FOUR

As a result of the tremendous chemical and electromagnetic changes taking place within your brain, you may suffer from headaches, blurred vision, weakened eyesight, or hearing difficulties as vision and hearing are 'retuned' in order to pick up the more subtle messages and tones informing the psyche and/or activating dormant 'seeds' of awakening. Energy levels can remain a challenge during Phase Four.

You might experience mild chest pains, bronchial infections, cardiac arrhythmias, increased pulse rate and/or higher or lower blood pressure as the heart chakra begins to open more fully and expand. (*Be sure to check any symptoms with the appropriate medical tests that often transpire to produce entirely 'normal' results).

During this Phase, you might also begin to experience an inexplicable compulsion to follow your heart, the seat of the soul, without question. Greater emphasis is placed on the purifying of your physical, emotional and mental bodies, and your energetic field. Your dietary choices change and you will eliminate stimulants such as tobacco and alcohol.

You transcend the need for psychotropics. You might also become free of a prior need/necessity for pharmaceuticals. You will most likely have adopted a vegan lifestyle at this stage. This is the phase where you begin to master the emotional body.

PHASE FIVE

During this Phase, the mental body begins to acquiesce to the wisdom of the heart and soul, from which it takes it primary directives. Lucid dreams, and déjà vu become increasingly frequent. Your thinking is now more non- linear. You begin to unhook from 3D conditioning and mentality.

Deprogramming from old thought patterns occurs exponentially as you begin to step out of the matrix and anchor into the 'heart grid' and 'light matrices' that overlay the Earth. You shift from 'reaction' (personality/ego/adapted self) to 'response' (healed and integrated ego, Authentic Self). You also prioritise 'BEing' over 'doing'. During this Phase you begin to master the mental body.

PHASE SIX

You attract those of similar vibration into your life. Many old friendships and contacts fall away as you have simply outgrown them in the process of manifesting like-minded/heart connected soul family and friends. You re-evaluate your life; including relationships, home, environment, and lifestyle preferences. You become aware of an increasing compulsion to fully release the past and write a new life story.

You relinquish the scripts handed to you by others or your ancestors. You move back and forth between clinging to the old comfort zones and letting these go. Fears will still surface but you are more able to view them as unfounded and rise above them. You feel elevated, lighter and freer.

At this stage, your body is capable of holding thirty-five percent light. Predominantly living by your intuition feels more natural now. You enter into the process of transcending the emotional body and locating in the realm of pure feeling.

PHASE SEVEN

The heart chakra further opens and expands. You live more and more from your heart, your soul, and your True Self. You are releasing deeper levels of emotional residues as you continue to transcend the emotional field in ways that maintain harmony within you and with others. You take full responsibility for your emotional 'reactions' and begin to experience a new lightness of being as your emotions become healed and you move into the vast and liberating expanse of pure feeling.

You lose your emotional attachment to others and preferred outcomes, as you begin to embrace a modus operandi of non-attachment. Headaches may continue to occur because of pressure on the pituitary and pineal glands as they further open and expand. This could disrupt sleep patterns and you may find that you are barely sleeping for weeks on end but are functioning surprisingly well. You could be awake for nights on end and then sleep for anything up to eighteen hours without waking.

Your relationship with Spirit deepens and you become increasingly aware of Spirit Beings working with you and walking beside you. You focus on creating a new experience of your life. You eat less and now prefer lighter (Light infused) foods. You drink water in preference to other beverages. At this stage, you have refrained from eating or drinking anything that is unnatural or a stimulant.

PHASE EIGHT

You wish to be purely of Service. The cerebrum - the 'sleeping giant' - within the brain becomes activated. Cranial expansion is common as seed crystals in the brow and recorder crystals in the right side of the brain are activated along with the eighth, ninth and tenth chakras. You are drawn to non-verbal metaphysical languages such as the Language of Light. The pineal and pituitary glands are changing shape and opening more fully to create the 'arc of the covenant' - a rainbow light that arcs over the top of the head to the third eye; its purpose being to translate intricate and complex high-frequency language and code.

Words become a secondary form of communication as you begin to think instead in geometries, tones and the abstract. You become aware of the vastness and multidimensionality of who you really are, and realise that the only person who can limit your true expression as an awakened soul in human form is yourself. You increasingly feel the need for prolonged silence in order to deeply regenerate and more clearly hear the voice of your soul and Spirit. You experience renewed inspiration for Life and begin to view it through the eyes of unconditional love. You cease to operate from obligation and any propensity for people-pleasing has fallen away.

Relationships become transparent and transpersonal. Others may feel confused or disoriented around you because your vibration has altered to such an extent that they can no longer hook into your 'personality', as it has been healed and integrated and therefore you are present as pure soul. Your sensitivity and awareness are acutely heightened. You remain fundamentally grounded and serene.

PHASE NINE

Decoding geometries is easier. Toning is absorbed at a cellular level. Your Consciousness starts to entrain with the 6th dimensional blueprint as it begins to overlay your 5th dimensional light-body. Your physical body may change shape and colour (e.g. becomes paler or darker) as shifts occur within your energy fields. You feel connected and interconnected with all life forms and beings.

The opinions of others are of no concern to you. You are free. Phase nine brings a greater descension of the Light-body into the physical form. You live as a free spirit on Earth and give fully of yourself as a divine instrument serving the highest good of all. This is the Phase when the extent to which you are aligned with SOURCE defines and determines your life, your income, your relationships - everything. Dissolution of the 3rd dimensional self occurs.

You liberate yourself from the ties that bind and the chains of the emotions and lower mind. You are centred in harmony, peace and joy. You disconnect from the consensus reality. The choices you make can seem perplexing to others as at this level of the ascension process you are entirely non-conformist.

From the 7th, 8th and 9th levels, your inner-Light is visibly radiating. You feel deeply connected, grounded, centred, and filled with purpose. You remain connected to and operate from SOURCE Consciousness.

Your intention and actions remain focused on the highest good of all – however others of a less awakened consciousness will not always understand your motivations. You embody the 'I Am'. The 7th, 8th and 9th phases are an ongoing unification process of becoming fully connected to the ultimate state of Being in human form - I AM.

PHASE TEN

Your human Consciousness has entrained with SOURCE Consciousness. You have transcended the genetic blueprint to that which is divine. Instant manifestation occurs. Bi-location and teleporting (reference my latest book to be published in Spring 2021) enter the realms of possibility.

The Merkabah (another name for the Lightbody) allows you to experience your multi-dimensionality and travel through multi-realities simultaneously. This is the Phase where the individual has transcended the 3D templates of 'age' and 'gender identification' as they evolve towards embodying a state of androgyny.

PHASE ELEVEN

The Lightbody is predominantly active and is connected to your physical body via 'spin points'. These are positioned within the 'Light-Grid' that overlays the acupuncture meridians of the physical body and Earth, and are composed of lines of light intersecting in intricate and intelligent geometries. These 'spin points' and 'lines' correlate with both physical and non-physical chakras located within the luminous energy field (aura), which are responsible for the operation of the 5th dimensional circulatory system of Light. You have transcended collective conditioning.

You no longer uphold or support dysfunctional societal systems and their programs such as the "aging" of the physical body, which is determined by the messages it receives from the cellular level. Time is no longer linear. You follow only the higher directive of your soul. You have transcended 'old paradigm spirituality' and are instead aligned with the most highly advanced spiritual truth. There is no separation between your Higher Self and Self, for your Higher Purpose and SOURCE-connected reality have merged.

In this 'frame' of Conscious awareness many 9th Phase beings will create new types of Light-based-technologies along with harmonious new systems of governance, finance and education, equitable food and resource allocation and distribution, evolved models for community living, and enlightened solutions to restore balance to humanity, Nature and the Earth. This is the directive of the Age of Aquarius – a Uranian Age now upon us.

PHASE TWELVE

Phase Twelve empowers the Higher Directive Creation impulse behind the vision and trajectories of Phases Nine to Eleven. This is when the physical implementation and manifestation of enlightened systems become firmly rooted and established. This phase represents the final initiation of 12th Phase beings; as creators, pioneers, visionaries, trailblazers, initiators and figureheads for the New and Future Earth. Many 12th Phase beings are from the Future and are already here now to sow the seeds of a future awakened epoch.

This is the Phase where the Divine Plan for Earth becomes accessible and the vision of an enlightened human race becomes accepted as the norm. At this final level of ascension beings hold 70% Light, and are present as 5th dimensional Consciousness serving multi-universal directives.

The ultimate awakened state of Self-transcendence has been embodied and the individual has attained the state of super-luminous androgyny. A youthful body is maintained and these beings are perceived as ageless. From a gender perspective they have also transcended the current identification program of 'male/female'. Their physical appearance will still be masculine or feminine but their Consciousness remains gender neutral.

Personal will has dissolved and merged with the Higher Will of the Soul and Divine Will. The Self, Higher Self and Soul are entrained with the Heart of the Cosmos and SOURCE.

Further Ascension Signs/Symptoms

The following is a list of other ascension phenomena you may or may not experience throughout the ascension process.

- An increase in psychic, mediumistic, clairvoyant, and intuitive skills.
- Acute aversion to negative energy, people or environments.

- Extreme sensitivity to being in public places or among groups of people and crowds.
- A preference for becoming more reclusive even though previously sociable.
- Sudden inexplicable anxiety attacks occurring at any time with no valid reason.
- Acute sensitivity to shopping malls or social environments such as restaurants, clubs, festivals, theatres, etc.
- Extreme sensitivity and intolerance to digital and wireless technology as well as artificial lighting.
- Zoning out for long periods (feeling out of it, which you literally are in those moments) – an overpowering need to do nothing as your Consciousness spends increasing amounts of time in the fifth-dimension.
- The need to rest or sleep for much longer periods than usual.
- Prolonged bouts of insomnia either up to or from 3:30 am - a sign of your Consciousness adapting to new cycles of activity and/or receiving new light-codes and galactic/solar downloads.
- Strange electrical sensations coursing through the body or body parts, such as legs or arms due to downloads of galactic frequencies flooding the planet with the purpose of 'rewiring' the circuitry of the physical and energy bodies, and the Lightbody, in order to withstand and entrain with the incoming higher vibrational energies.
- Numerous physical symptoms caused by the detoxification of the body as it continues to release physical, emotional, mental, psychological, karmic and ancestral toxins.
- Dizziness, balance problems, and feeling spacey, triggered by dipping in and out of higher states of Consciousness and/or activity within or in relation to the planets and the etheric poles.
- Increased and decreased appetite. Either putting on or losing weight no matter how much or little you eat, which

is due to the effects of the body shifting from third to fifth-dimensional chemistry.

- Transitional symptoms (from 3D-5D consciousness) including shaking, heavy limbs, weakness, high-pitched ringing in ears, heart palpitations, headaches, coughing, compressed/tight chest feeling, sensation of skin tingling or burning; frequent visits to the bathroom to clear through bowel and urination, nausea for several days at a time with no other accompanying symptoms, muscle aches, blurred vision, unclear thinking, exhaustion, washed out looking/pale, changes within the tone of voice as it re-pitches on a deeper or higher scale, skin anomalies such as rashes, sudden dry or red patches, lumps and bumps that appear for a while and then disappear, sweating, overheating, or cold to the extent of not being able to get warm, insomnia, excessive mucus and saliva, etc.

**As a precaution always seek medical advice in regard to any symptom of particular concern in case the cause is one that needs medical attention.

Teaching Four - The Diamond Heart Prayers

These Prayers can set forth our deepest soul intention and facilitate us to live joyful and liberated lives. They convey to the psyche, the body, (including energetic), emotions and mind, our most heartfelt wish to free ourselves from all that keeps us locked into suffering.

When stated with reverence and the deepest sincerity they can support us to move beyond seeming impediments such as karma, psychological wounding and the type of soul contracts and bonds we may experience as challenging.

Ultimately all such experiences are in service of our highest good and these Prayers can facilitate accelerated release, healing, integration and transcendence.

Free audio mp3 downloads of the Prayers can be found on my website – www.nicolyachristi.love. The frequency, tone and sound vibration of my voice transmitting the Prayers is highly conducive for it is infused with my energetic soul signature and pure and pristine higher-dimensional Intelligences that wish to support you.

The Diamond Heart Prayer
Meditation & Affirmation

These two special Prayers are powerful facilitators for transformation and transcendence.

Each Prayer is a spiritual mantra and acts in a similar way to a high vibrational tuning fork.

Engage personally with the Prayers as a Divine Medicine.

Recite them at sacred ceremonies.

Share them with friends.

Offer them to clients.

Intone them within groups.

Transmit them to large audiences at gatherings and events.

THE DIAMOND HEART PRAYER MEDITATION

With all of my Heart, I release all past-life debts, burdens, karma, vows, agreements, contracts, promises and bonds. I request that all such be lifted from my soul contract and dissolved and transmuted in the Divine Light and Love of Source.

With all of my Heart, I release all future life debts, burdens, karma, vows, agreements, contracts, promises and bonds. I request that all such be lifted from my soul contract and dissolved and transmuted in the Divine Light and Love of Source.

With all of my Heart, I request that all layers of my energy field are cleared and that all blocks within it are removed, dissolved and transmuted in the Divine Light and Love of Source.

With all of my Heart, I request that all defences, scars, karma, and blocks be lifted from my Heart and dissolved and transmuted in the Divine Light and Love of Source.

With all of my Heart, I request that all trauma memories from all incarnations be lifted from my soul memory and dissolved and transmuted in the Divine Light and Love of Source.

With all of my Heart, I request that all blocked or negative energies stored anywhere within my physical body and my energy bodies be removed, dissolved and transmuted in the Divine Light and Love of Source.

With all of my Heart, I request forgiveness for all transgressions - past, present and future - and that these be lifted from my soul memory and dissolved and transmuted in the Divine Light and Love of Source.

With all of my Heart, I request that all cellular memory and genetic DNA be wiped clean of all trauma imprints and negative energies and that these be flooded with and hold only the purest and highest vibrational Love and Light.

With all of my Heart, I request that my life now begins to reflect only the greatest and purest Love and Light, and that I live in unconditional love, flow, joy, vibrancy, magic, wonder, wellness, positivity, happiness, fun, perfect balance, adventure, purity and true abundance.

With all of my Heart, I ask that my heart become peaceful, that I become joy-full, and perfectly centred and anchored in Love. That the Light and Love of my soul's divine essence pours through my heart, my eyes, my smile, my very Being.

With all of my Heart, I request that I become the embodiment of Peace and Love, and that I come to know the most exalted and purest expression of Unconditional Love, and that I express this to and for all of humanity, all sentient Beings, and all life forms, in all realms of the Earth.

With all of my Heart, I request that from this day forward I am gifted with the greatest experiences of Love, Joy, Happiness, Laughter, Peace, Blessedness, Beauty, and True Abundance and Fulfilment.

With all of my Heart, I request that my life be one that is blessed from this moment forth.

With all of my Heart, I request that I come to fully know and experience true, deep, sacred and abiding Love.

With all of my Heart, I request that I take with me a treasure trove of unforgettable, magical, and beautiful memories, when it is time for me to return HOME.

THE DIAMOND HEART PRAYER AFFIRMATION

I choose only to live from the Love that I AM.

I choose only to love from the Light that I AM.

I choose only to speak from the Understanding that I AM.

I choose only to hear from the Compassion that I AM.

I choose only to see from the Beauty that I AM.

I choose only to unconditionally love from the Unconditional Love that I AM.

I choose that my every thought, word, action and deed be in alignment with the Truth of who I AM.

The River of LOVE that I AM never ceases to flow.

The Temple of my Heart is a Refuge and Sanctuary for all sentient beings and all life on Earth.

I live in the Present - The Moment - The Now - lovingly accepting What Is, not what has been, or is yet to come.

Each day I renew a vow to LOVE all I encounter, be that human, winged, furred, insect, plant, mineral, and elemental.

Each day I renew a vow to respond and not to react.

I hold an attitude of unconditional positive regard for all.

I cultivate peace in every step, with every breath, in every thought, word, action and deed.

I AM PEACE.

I AM: Compassion, Empathy, Beauty, Joy, Humility, Grace and Reverence.

Each day I pause to appreciate and experience the Wonder of this Gift called Life.

Today is the first day of the rest of my life.

I live in Gratitude.

I live as Pristine Truth.

My Heart is a Diamond.

I radiate Purest Love.

I Am Peace.

I AM That I AM.

I AM.

LOVE.

About The Author

Nicolya Christi is a Visionary, Futurist, Published Author and Writer.

Her first book **'2012: A Clarion Call:** *Your Soul's Purpose in Conscious Evolution'* (Bear & Co/Inner Traditions - April 2011), was placed in the top ten book reviews by Publishers Weekly in Spring 2011. Professor Ervin Laszlo, twice nominated for the Nobel Peace Prize, stated: *This is the most remarkable spiritual book on this or any other subject I have ever read.* Satish Kumar noted: *Nicolya Christi is a Visionary and Thinker and Writer and her work in articulating and promoting conscious evolution is outstanding.* Barbara Marx Hubbard who penned the Foreword wrote: *Nicolya Christi is our guide through this evolutionary world shift and one of the best I have encountered.*

Her second book, **'Contemporary Spirituality for an Evolving World:** *A Handbook for Conscious Evolution'* (Bear & Co/Inner Traditions September 2013) is endorsed by Barbara Marx Hubbard, Larry Dossey M.D., Pierre Pradervand, and the Rev. Peter Owen-Jones. Ervin Laszlo wrote the foreword.

Nicolya's third mainstream book (title forthcoming) is to be published by Inner Traditions/Bear & Co/Findhorn Press and will be available online and in English language bookstores worldwide from Autumn 2021. It is endorsed by several luminaries including Bruce H Lipton, Jean Houston, Masami Sajioni and Emmanuel Dagher.

She is also just completing a new pocketbook title: **'Meditation__365:** *Daily Meditations, Contemplations,*

Affirmations & Inspirations' (Waterside Press) which will be available from November 2020.

Nicolya has contributed to several other books including: **'2013 - The Beginning is Now'** (Spring 2011) with contemporaries including Jose Arguelles, Geoff Stray, Carl Johan Calleman, Jim Young and Gill Edwards: **'Dawn of the Akashic Age'** (Spring 2013) by Ervin Laszlo and Kingsley Dennis: **'Beyond Rage & Fear'** (Spring 2017) along with authors including Jean Houston, Stanislav Grof and Gary Zukav: And **'Reconnecting With The Source'**, (2020) by Ervin Laszlo with contributors including Jane Goodall and James O'Dea.

Nicolya is currently writing her first novel - a sweeping fiction-based-on-fact account of two history defining timelines and the convergence of the evolutionary *call* of both of these in the here and now. The story conveys a critical message for humanity in these pivotal, precarious and yet highly auspicious times in terms of the ultimate transgression of millennia of 'power-over' rule and the establishing of a new conscious epoch founded on the **Power of Love**.

Nicolya Christi's Work is founded on three fundamental principles: *Psychological Integration, Conscious Evolution* and *Spiritual Awakening*, with a core focus on spirituality, metaphysics, philosophy and psychology.

Over the last ten years she has developed various *psycho-spiritual maps and models for evolving consciousness* and continues to bring unique new theories to the psychological and spiritual domains all of which are inspired by extensive experience in these fields.

Between June 1997 and November 2002 she experienced over five years of out-of-body experiences (OBE's), which included mystical and futuristic encounters with otherworldly realities and a life-changing experience of conscious dying in March 2002. In October 2009 she had a consciousness transforming and existence defining experience of Enlightenment.

www.nicolyachristi.love

About The Author